Boise State University Western Writers Series

Dee Brown

By Lyman B. Hagen

Arkansas State University

Editors: Wayne Chatterton
James H. Maguire

Business Manager:
James Hadden

Cover Design and Illustration
by Arny Skov, Copyright 1990

Boise State University, Boise, Idaho

Copyright 1990
by the
Boise State University Western Writers Series

ALL RIGHTS RESERVED

Library of Congress Card No. 90-80260

International Standard Book No. 0-88430-094-3

Printed in the United States of America by
Boise State University Printing and Graphics Services
Boise, Idaho

Dee Brown

Dee Brown

In 1974, *Choice* magazine voiced a widely held opinion when it characterized Dee A. Brown as "a distinguished writer of Western history" (284). By then he had also become known to a wide audience as a first-rate storyteller. Yet prior to the publication in 1970 of *Bury My Heart at Wounded Knee*, he had labored in relative obscurity, athough writing a steady stream of novels, articles, and historical reference books. Then the success and acceptance of *Bury My Heart* lifted him to national prominence.

Born in Alberta, Louisiana, on 28 February 1908, Dee Brown was one of four children of Daniel Alexander, a lumberman, and Lulu Cranford Brown. When Dee was five, his father died and the family moved to the maternal grandmother's in Stephens, Arkansas. In Stephens his mother supported the family from her wages; and while she worked, her mother looked after the children. Grandmother Cranford exercised considerable influence on Brown's intellectual and emotional development. She remembered family and friends who followed the California Gold Rush, she had driven an ox wagon to Arkansas, and she could recall the Civil War in detail, since her husband served in it. One of her first projects with young Dee was to teach him to read. Stories were an important part of their relationship. At that time, Arkansas touched on the Southwest frontier and was peopled by many who knew first-hand the events of the westward expansion. Thus Brown had an early association with tales of the Old West, and the seeds of an interest in that era were planted. Later in life, he seemed naturally inclined to focus on stories of the latter half of the nineteenth century and the frontier lands of that time.

Brown is one of a group of Arkansas writers who grew up knowing they were treading Indian lands and walking through real places of Western frontier history. Brown and his neighbors Douglas Jones and Charles Portis each realized he often walked in his youth parts of the Trail of Tears, the great Indian Nation Reservation, the Quapaw Quarter, the Osage village, the Creek settlements, and Ft. Smith, the base of infamous hanging judge Isaac Parker.

Brown received his elementary education in the small-town Arkansas schools in Stephens. Of those formative years, Brown says he is glad he "was lucky enough to grow up in an Arkansas town in the beginning of this century" ("Growing Up" 19A). He feels the rural family atmosphere was nurturing. When he reached the age of fourteen, he and a cousin bought a hand press and produced a successful weekly paper. They initially wrote a series of stories about the local Boy Scouts. An oil boom was in progress in that part of Arkansas (El Dorado and Stephens), and Scout troops had been organized to provide a wholesome activity for the sons of the oil workers. Even then, Brown showed a social conscience in his articles and editorials, condemning the practices of the "booming oil business." He has said he felt "the land was being assassinated" (Courtemanche-Ellis 556). Oil was being dumped indiscriminately, destroying streams and trees. The industry was a major employer of Indians in its fields and on its rigs, and many of the Indian children were friends of Dee Brown. Brown and a pal, who happened to be an Indian boy, haunted the Saturday movie matinees, the cowboy and Indian pictures so popular at the time. His friend convinced him that the screen portrayals they saw were far from true depictions of real Indians. The boys were entertained by the movies, but were not taken in by the myths foisted on the public. Brown learned that historical accuracy was not always a part of popular stories, and he developed an independence in doing research and in forming opinions. He decided he wanted to find out all he could about something to get to the "real truth" (personal interview).

Brown attended high school in Little Rock, Arkansas. He studied printing in his senior year and learned to set type and run a linotype. After graduation, he could not find a job in Little Rock, but the Harrison, Arkansas, *Daily Times* offered him work as a printer and part-time reporter. During his brief tenure, he filed some interesting local stories and became a regional correspondent for the *Arkansas Gazette*, the Memphis' *Commercial Appeal*, the *St. Louis Post Dispatch*, and the *Kansas City Star*. Deciding that he needed more education to be a good reporter, Brown enrolled for the winter term of 1928 at Arkansas State Teachers College in Conway (Shiras 13A). He worked in the college library to earn expense money and in the process learned many of the skills of library work. Brown graduated in June of 1931 with an A.B. in Education that included concentrations in History and English.

Between terms during high school and college, Brown and a few friends had set out in an old Ford to explore Oklahoma and other Western states, visiting historical sites and whatever intrigued them. By the time of his college graduation, they had covered the West. On one trip, a young teacher, who had written about the Mormon Trail for his doctoral dissertation, lectured the group during their touring, and that summer Brown learned much about the West (Saltz 9E2).

Graduating from college during the Great Depression, Brown found it hard to get a job in Arkansas. He headed for Washington, D.C., where he had better luck being hired. But over the next three years, he worked at around fifty different jobs (*Current Biography* 51). In 1934, he passed a Civil Service exam that resulted in an entry-level position as an assistant librarian in the United States Department of Agriculture. That same year, Brown married Sara Baird Stroud, who had gone to college with him in Arkansas. They subsequently had two children, a son and a daughter.

Brown decided to follow a career in librarianship and, while still with the Department of Agriculture, earned a B.L.S. degree in 1937 from George Washington University. Two years later, he became librarian of the department's Beltsville Research Center in Beltsville, Maryland, and he remained there until he was drafted into the Army in 1942. After being assigned to the 80th Infantry Division in Tennessee, he was transferred to special services for library-related work in the National Archives in the Washington, D.C., area. He was discharged in 1945 with the rank of Sergeant (*Current Biography* 51).

Upon leaving the service, Brown became a librarian for the Technical Information Branch Library at the U.S. Army's Aberdeen Proving Grounds in Aberdeen, Maryland (Courtemanche-Ellis 556). He served at that post from 1945 until 1948, at which time he joined the staff of the University of Illinois library. In 1951 he earned an M.S. degree from the University of Illinois. He served as librarian for the College of Agriculture until his retirement in 1972 (Bevilacqua 143). During his tenure at Illinois, he edited the journal *Agricultural History* from 1956 through 1958 and held the rank of Professor in the library school from 1962. Upon retirement, Brown returned to Arkansas and took up residence in Little Rock, where he hopes to live out his days in relative peace and quiet (personal interview).

Dee Brown has been writing regularly for publication since the 1930s. His newspaper work sharpened his natural skills and developed his awareness of writing markets. He submitted articles and short stories to a variety of magazines such as *Hinterland* and *Esquire*, and he often wrote about subjects he had known personally such as the lives of sharecroppers or the pains of picking cotton. In a 1937 article published in the *Christian Science Monitor*, he advocated the industrialization of American farming (Courtemanche-Ellis 556).

When his short story about a drive-in restaurant won a prize, it attracted the attention of the New York literary agents McIntosh and Otis. They contacted Brown, who was living in Washington, D.C., at the time, and they asked if he had written any longer works. Brown replied affirmatively and rapidly put together a satire about the Washington bureaucracy. Macrae-Smith Company of Philadelphia agreed to publish it. The Japanese bombed Pearl Harbor before the book had been printed, however; and America's entry into the war made inappropriate the publication of material critical of the government. Brown's editor was nevertheless sufficiently impressed by his work to ask for anything else he might have, and Brown worked furiously to turn out *Wave High the Banner* (1942), a novel based on the life of Davy Crockett. Thus was Dee Brown launched as a writer of books.

In the almost five decades since *Wave High* appeared, Brown has written a considerable body of work, both fiction and nonfiction, that has secured for him a reputation as an award-winning author who appeals to a wide audience, including Civil War and Western buffs, high school students, children, and even collectors of "coffee table" volumes. Throughout all Brown's books, his strengths of careful research and imaginative presentation are apparent. Winifred F. Bevilacqua calls him "a gifted raconteur who narrates his stories in an informative and entertaining manner" (147). Brown says his focus upon the Civil War and Western expansion reflects his personal interests and heritage (personal interview). In his casual reading of historical documents, old newspapers, and diaries, he has frequently uncovered an incident worthy of development into a book.

Dee Brown has written that "the first requirement for anyone who aspires to the writing of historical fiction is to be born with, or to acquire, a fondness for a certain period and place in our past" ("Historical" 12). His own books bear out his belief that total immersion in the era of one's choice is a requisite to validly portraying an event set in that period. He is one of a select group of writers whose careful, detailed research has imparted to their written works an air of authenticity. Surrounded by the detail of the story, a reader of a Dee Brown book knows the exact setting, the terrain, the weather conditions, the placement of characters, the social motivations of characters, and the expected responses and reactions. Brown makes his readers participants in his stories by drawing them into the details of each scene. Although his prose, particularly his constructed dialogue, is not always sparkling, his readers nevertheless find themselves intrigued with the information on each page and compelled to see how this or that detail weighs upon the outcome of the tale. Readers of any of Dee Brown's books, whether fiction or non-fiction, put them down convinced that whatever they have just read has told them exactly how things happened.

In "Historical Fiction, Its Infinite Variety," Brown makes his case for the essentialness of verity in research. Apparently, he has been little influenced by the market forces dictated by publishers of Western fiction (forces identified in Christine Bold's *Selling the Wild West*). Although Brown has been quoted as being inspired to write for the extra income (Courtemanche-Ellis 558), only *Yellowhorse* (1956), *Cavalry Scout* (1958), and *The Girl from Fort Wicked* (1964) can be categorized as formula Westerns. Brown seems first to have chosen his stories and then to have taken his chances on their acceptance by publishers and public. He provides an unvarnished presentation of his Western subject matter by using diaries, newspapers, maps, and other primary source materials to capture the language and tone of the period about which he is writing. He has said, "I have studied a single photograph by the hour to absorb the atmosphere of a time and a place" ("Historical" 12).

In spite of his attempts to achieve authenticity, Brown's early works received mixed reviews. He was, for example, roundly scored by Paul Engle in a review of *Wave High the Banner:*

> There is little of the "tall tale" quality; the wild humor and the exaggerated deed have been cut out. What is left is a more straightforward, cleaned-up story, lacking the zest and vigor of the original. (9)

Margaret Wallace, on the other hand, reviewing the same novel, apparently recognized Brown's method of presentation and reported, "It is told in an idiom not far removed from that which Crockett himself might have commanded . . . . Dialogue and details of background are uniformly excellent" (16).

Over four decades later, the historical consensus suppported Wallace's assessment of *Wave High*. In August 1986, at a meeting in Tennessee, about two dozen revisionist historians gathered for a one-day symposium called "New Perspectives on the Man [Davy Crockett] and the Myth." The researchers talked about Crockett as a "literary archetype" and proceeded to reveal newly unearthed information that reduced the real David Crockett to his genuine status as a mere mortal (Pasztor B1). The literary critic John Seelye attributed the Crockett legend to profit-motivated Boston publishers of numerous almanacs of the 1830s and 1840s. Thus it appears that Dee Brown wrote an accurate account of the man David

Crockett and was fully justified in not furthering the tall-tale image.

Such hindsight may eventually offset negative reviews such as Engle's, but Brown's reputation continues to be shadowed by those unfavorable views of his early work. William Bloodworth, for example, contends that Brown produced "unspectacular and relatively unnoticed novels about particular Western individuals," until his fiction really came of age in *Creek Mary's Blood* (122). But instead of Brown's work changing, it may well be that—after the popular success of *Bury My Heart* and subsequent historical writing—what came of age was an appreciation of Brown's writing.

Engle's lack of appreciation of *Wave High* failed to shake Brown's conviction that thorough research is essential to good historical fiction, and Brown continued both his systematic and serendipitous research. While still on Army duty, Brown and a colleague, Martin L. Schmitt, were assigned to search for military photographs in the files of the National Archives. They found themselves in the midst of a vast trove of Americana. Using their spare time to collect and annotate faded pictures of the Old West that had been tucked away in the Archives and were in danger of being lost to the public, the two men were able to assemble enough materials to provide the basis for three profusely illustrated volumes of the westward movement of the nineteenth century. These pictures fell into three categories, representing separate entities of the movement: the Indians, the cowboys, and the settlers. Schmitt chose the photographs and Brown prepared the accompanying text. The collaborators secured approval for publication of their three volumes by Scribner's famed editor, Maxwell Perkins. Additional pictures were found by Brown and Schmitt in state historical society records, mainly those of Kansas and Nebraska, and in private collections and other sources of photographs. The first volume of the trilogy, *Fighting Indians of the West*, was published by Scribner's in 1949.

Brown realized the importance and quality of the early photographs they had collected and accordingly gave credit to the early photographers.

Fighting Indians contains some 270 photographs, paintings, and drawings of the persons and places involved in the Indian wars of the West. Oliver La Farge labels the book an "eminently successful" pictorial history that "honestly and dispassionately" tells a great story (6). Hoffman Birney claims *Fighting Indians* is "one of the most valuable single contributions to frontier history that has been made in more than a quarter-century" (5).

Trail Driving Days, the second book of the series, was published in 1952. It also contained over two hundred pictures, this time covering "every phase of driving meat on the hoof from the ranges to the railheads," according to the *New Yorker* reviewer who found the book to be "fascinating" (96). Hoffman Birney again thought the series "an absolute must for any library of the West" (18). *Time* magazine reported, "some of the stories . . . have been told before, but seldom if ever have so many good ones been strung together with honest-looking pictures. The result is a book that takes the old West away from the spurious Westerns and gives it back to the real cowmen and bad men" (104).

The last of the three pictorial books, *The Settlers' West*, was released by Scribner's in 1955. This volume includes pictures, sketches, and text chronicling the events of the actual settling of the frontier lands. Portraying the variety of people, from sodbusters to land agents to pioneer business and professional men, *Settlers' West* completes the history of the era Brown and Schmitt wanted to preserve for the American public.

During the Army Archives period, while searching for the military photographs he had been assigned to find, Brown also came across much Civil War period material. His earlier interest in that time increased, and he focused on cavalry operations. While rummaging around the document files, Brown read a report about a foray of a Union Army brigade led by one Colonel Benjamin H. Grierson. This Illinois unit had made a remarkable sixteen-day, six-hundred-mile sweep from La Grange, Tennessee, its staging area, across the state of Mississippi, killing and wounding about a hundred enemy soldiers, freeing over five hundred Union prisoners, and destroying miles of Confederate telegraph lines before ending at Baton Rouge, Louisiana. The raid also destroyed "over 3,000 stands of arms, and other army stores and government property to an immense amount. The losses incurred by Grierson were small" (Woody 688). Brown learned that the Colonel was a most unlikely leader for such a successful raid, or for such a unit. Grierson had been an Illinois music teacher who hated horses. After going to work for the University of Illinois, Brown recalled reading about Grierson's unit and decided to see what more he could learn about it. His research uncovered an unpublished autobiography by Grierson himself and a store of family journals and papers. Using what he found, Brown wrote a factual, diary-form book, *Grierson's Raid* (1954), tracing the daily activities of the unit. The book was well-received by reviewers. J.K. Bettersworth commented: " . . . Civil War fact has hardly been so imaginatively handled since the days of Stephen Vincent Benét" (26). And B.P. Thomas noted, "The story has needed telling and Brown does it adroitly" (6).

Brown showed a balanced approach toward the soldiers of the Civil War when he wrote *The Bold Cavaliers: Morgan's 2nd Kentucky Cavalry Raid* (1959). Here he told the story of a hard-fighting, intrepid Confederate Army unit under the command of John Hunt Morgan. These Kentucky troopers ranged through several states doing battle with Union troops from 1861 to 1865. Brown has noted that nineteenth-century newspapers and unpublished diaries were his primary sources for the writing of this book (Courtemanche-Ellis, "Dee Brown" 13).

All of Dee Brown's work has included his accounts of actual events that he has uncovered during his research. Even when he turned to stock Western fiction as in *Yellowhorse* (1956) and *Cavalry Scout* (1958), he used actual happenings as important parts of his plots. Official data from the files of the old Army Balloon Corps provide the important element of surprise in *Yellowhorse*. Hoffman Birney, reviewing the novel, acknowledges it as an "exuberant yarn" of cavalry versus Indians, with the "established props—the impetuous colonel, his cheating wife, . . . the rancher's daughter, . . . an old enlisted guide." He questions the authenticity of the balloon incident (26), but Brown insists it is documented (personal interview).

As Brown's first Western novel, *Yellowhorse* incorporates four literary practices common to formula Westerns. First, the setting is the Western frontier in the latter half of the nineteenth century; second, the plot contains conflict, with various chases, escapes, and rescues, and a unique event; third, the subject matter somehow involves Indians; and fourth, historical authenticity is emphasized. Brown generally follows these conventions in his works. Although his books were written and published in the post-World War II era, Brown did not forsake the conventional hero and heroine or follow many contemporary authors who acceded to popular demands for sex and gratuitous violence. His *Yellowhorse* presents an honorable, cultivated, handsome hero, Captain Thomas Jefferson Easterwood, who, by wisdom and ingenuity, overcomes a series of conflicts. A faithful guide and a previously befriended Indian chief help the good captain save not only a prominent rancher's family but also Fort Yellowhorse and the troopers of the fort. The yarn builds to an exciting climax when a weather balloon is launched to frighten attacking Indians away from Fort Yellowhorse.

The trick succeeds, the hero marries the rancher's beautiful daughter, evil-doers suffer, and the good live happily ever after.

Yellowhorse contains more similes than can be found in later works by Brown. He is apparently experimenting with his narrative style in an attempt to capture the tone and flavor he found in newspapers and journals of the Old West. Sentences such as "The buffalo are become as few as raindrops in the moons of summer" (24), and "This country was as peaceful as a New England meadow" (4), will seldom be found in subsequent novels. Brown's evolving deceptively simple, straightforward narrative style accommodates readers of many ages and allows the events, the action, to dominate his stories.

Yellowhorse and Brown's next novel, *Cavalry Scout* (1958), were well-structured tales that satisfied a reader by offering high adventure and good conquering evil. Like many of Brown's books, *Yellowhorse* went through a number of printings and was eventually reissued in paperback.

Doubleday originally published a pair of Brown's stories—*The Girl from Fort Wicked* (1964) and *Action at Beecher Island* (1967)—in its series of Double D Brand Westerns. *Fort Wicked* opens with the robbery of an Army payroll from a stagecoach. The passengers are brutally murdered and thus begins a vendetta between the book's hero, a stalwart cavalry captain, and an evil squaw-man who lures renegade Arapahoes into doing his dirty deeds. The captain's bride-to-be is one of the stagecoach victims, and part of the story concerns his dealing with anger and pain arising from his loss. A young girl left to the care of a kindly trading-post couple becomes the central character in the story. The wild, free-spirited girl develops into a socialized woman through the effects of the goodness she receives from others. Brown includes much suspense and action with clashes between troopers and Indians. In the end, with the girl's help, the captain is avenged. Good is rewarded and evil punished, but not without sacrifice. *Fort Wicked* is fiction, but the stagecoach robbery and murders had been reported in old newspapers Brown uncovered. The novel's bereaved captain is based upon an actual person, but the other characters were created by Brown.

The other Double D Brand Western, *Action at Beecher Island* (1967), is "neither fiction, nor completely non-fiction," according to *Publishers Weekly* ("Action at Beecher Island" 82), although it is reviewed under the non-fiction classification. This confusion is a natural reaction to Brown's occasional practice of combining bits of actual historical information when he tells what his research and moral intuition convince him is the true story of an event. *Beecher Island* is an example of such slightly fictionalized history. The story recounts the nine-day siege of Forsyth's Scouts, a hand-picked band of fifty-one brave frontiersmen organized to locate a large Indian war party believed to be gathering. Although Major George (Sandy) Forsyth leads the unit, the operation is primarily a civilian endeavor. The Indians turn the tables and force the scouts to retreat to tiny Beecher Island in the Republican River. The ensuing battle is regarded by some historians as the greatest Indian fight of all. Brown structures *Beecher Island* so that each chapter covers the activities of a specific time period from the point of view of an individual Scout or Indian involved in the action. These participants recall the experience with differing perspectives and thus provide a well-rounded assessment for the reader. Again, diaries, official reports, personal letters, newspapers of the time, and oral recollections give Brown the basic material from which to weave his story. The suspense inherent in the situation captures readers from the beginning, and Brown's multi-faceted presentation pulls readers into the excitement and terror of the action rather than encouraging them to sit in judgment of those involved in the event.

As his authorial career proceeded, Brown showed an increasing sympathy for all who suffered during the settlement of the West. His major theme has been the injustice of the Old West, and while he has focused mainly on the injustice suffered by the Indians, he has also shown that farmers, soldiers, railroad workers, and women have been the victims of injustice. He shines a bright light on perpetrators of greed, treachery, and inhumanity. And he finds ordinary and extraordinary people who deserve praise and acknowledgment for their virtue. His values are rooted in solid Bible-Belt America.

Raised by his widowed mother and his grandmother, Brown had witnessed the strengths and endurance, not to mention the intelligence and ingenuity, of women. His grandmother had told him many stories of frontier adventures, some of these involved her women friends who had gone west on wagon trains (personal interview). Brown had come to feel that the "sun-bonnet myth" (*Current Biography* 53) failed to tell the real story of the pioneer women. He therefore picked an assortment of twenty-five women he felt presented a cross-section of the influence wielded by females on the frontier, and from a very large but neglected reservoir of diaries, letters, newspaper clippings, registries, historical society records, and eye-witness reports, he reconstructed the trails they had followed and the trials they had endured. He titled his narrative *The Gentle Tamers: Women of the Old Wild West* (1958), "one of his first books to achieve national acclaim . . ." ("Dee Brown," *Arkansas Times* 57). His chapters structured arbitrary groupings of settlers, army wives, missionaries, teachers, courtesans, and entertainers (Bevilacqua 144). The well-known personalities such as Calamity Jane, Belle Starr, Elizabeth Custer, and Lola Montez were of no more significance than their sisters of lesser fame such as Frances Grumman, widow of the Fetterman Massacre, or Loretta Velasquez, who had fought in the Civil War disguised as a man but who attacked the frontier in full-blown womanly glory. Although popular and generally well reviewed, *Gentle Tamers* received some criticism for the omission of well-known frontier figures such as Sacagewea and Jessie Fremont ("Gentle Tamers," *Kirkus* 111). Overall, however, critics praised *Gentle Tamers* as a "well-researched, wittily written 'contribution to Americana' " (*Current Biography* 53), and it has never been out of print.

Gentle Tamers did not initiate the historical study of Western women. In 1944, Nancy Wilson Ross wrote admiringly of a select group of Western heroines. Her *Westward the Women* and *Heroines of the Early West* utilized much the same type of research material that Brown used in *Gentle Tamers*. However, Ross dealt with far more familiar figures such as Sacagewea, Narcissa Whitman, Abigail Scott Duniway, Eliza Spalding, and Mary Walker. Gentler in tone, Ross's work confines itself to the upright souls. In contrast, Brown includes in *Gentle Tamers* women who might be regarded as adventurers and perhaps even rogues. He writes with more humor than Ross, but in no way does he fail to admire the accomplishments of the frontier woman, great or small.

Although Brown is a gentle man who readily champions women and others who have suffered neglect and injustice, he also has a mild mischievous streak that sometimes comes out in interviews when he expresses his strong opinions about a variety of his peeves. He pokes fun at whatever crosses his mind at the moment, and his satirical comments are effective. His easy, disarming sense of humor contrasts with his deliberate factual tabulations. Only once during his career has Brown turned loose his humor and let his imagination fashion a satirical novel, *They Went Thataway* (1960).

Drawing upon his experiences in the Department of Agriculture in the 1930s and in the academic world of the 1950s, Brown incorporated into *They Went Thataway* gentle swipes at two of his pet peeves: the silliness and narrowness of some academic scholarship, and the swollen bureaucracy in Washington, D.C.

Because the central character, Philip Faraday, is an academic—a history professor and doctoral candidate—and because much of the action takes place on academic turf, this spoof belongs in the genre of the academic novel. But Brown never completely departs from his familiar nineteenth-century West, because the subject of Philip Faraday's doctoral research is a nineteenth-century military officer, General Charles Crawford Comstock ("Old Lightning and Grits"), and the massacre of his troops at the battle of Crazy Creek. General Comstock is an obvious replica of George Armstrong Custer, and the battle of Crazy Creek is patterned after the battle of the Little Big Horn. Brown adjusts circumstances to fit the plan of his fiction, however, and at the novel's end, we learn that Comstock didn't disobey orders to engage in battle as General Custer is alleged to have done.

The entire cast of characters in *Thataway* is a bizarre band: a fast-talking Hollywood director and producer, Benny Valodon; a scholar with a pretentious name, Dr. Henry Patrick Kilbourne; a television personality newspaperman, Lars Flensing; a ballet dancer; and assorted intelligence and Pentagon officers. This varied group succumbs to the traditional literary devices of farce: mistaken identity and misinterpretation. In fact, the entire, complicated plot turns on misinterpretation. Faraday's research subject, General Comstock, is confused with a current secret government project code-named Comstock. This leads to the mistaken notion that Faraday is a foreign agent. The government's Comstock project turns out to be a national park development, hardly a proper target for international intrigue. A classic farce with false deductions logically emerging from equally false premises, *Thataway* ultimately untangles its involved web of humorous complexities and ends with all put right—or at least properly sorted out. Brown's story-telling capability makes the novel exciting, not-so-preposterous, and funny. He himself liked it well enough to have it revived by August House, a select, non-profit Little Rock publisher, in 1984, under the title *Pardon My Pandemonium*.

The title for *Pandemonium* had been suggested by Brown's teenage grandson, for whom *They Went Thataway* was a favorite story. The narratives of Brown's books are easily read and followed by a young audience as well as by more mature readers, and in the sixties and seventies, Brown wrote several books intended specifically for the juvenile trade. *Showdown at Little Big Horn* (1964), a uniquely constructed account of General George Armstrong Custer's last campaign, follows the day-by-day preparations of the Seventh Cavalry for battle, the movement of the troops, and the battle engagements. Brown traces individual participants each step of the way. *Showdown* is not, however, meant to be a definitive history such as Quentin Reynold's *Custer's Last Stand* (1951) or Shannon Garst's *Custer, Fighter of the Plains* (1944). But Brown used the diaries, reports, and letters of the soldiers, civilians, and Indians involved in the epic encounter to provide the materials for an accurate, engrossing account tailored for a young audience.

Another book for children, *Andrew Jackson and the Battle of New Orleans* (1972), is Brown's carefully detailed history of the events culminating in Old Hickory's triumph over the British forces in the final battle of the War of 1812. The book recalls the patriotism of the pirate Jean Laffitte and the important role his men played in saving New Orleans. Young readers might have some difficulty following the rather complicated politics forged by a war of survival, but the story explains an important bit of American history. The ingenuity and determination of the American forces are bound to impress adolescent readers.

Brown stayed with Putnam's juvenile series for his 1973 *Tales of the Warrior Ants,* a rather bizarre conglomerate of information. Incorporating a classic short story by Carl Stephenson and writings from Mark Twain and several explorers and scientists, this narrative details the life-structure and habits of various strains of warrior ants. As an agricultural librarian, Brown had acquired considerable knowledge about such plagues and natural disasters visited upon farmers and planters. Although he rarely uses this specialized information as a basis for a book, he also wrote a biography, *James L. Reid, the Man and his Corn* (1955).

Brown's interest in providing good books for children prompted him to put together a gem of a book, *Tepee Tales of the American Indian* (1979). Brown realized that hundreds of marvelous Indian legends and myths were hidden away in obscure museum or governmental collections. He knew personally some of the individuals who had carefully preserved these stories and knew of most of the others, and he credits all the collectors for their dedication and foresight. From over one thousand tales Brown scanned—from sources such as the Field Columbian Museum in Chicago, the Carnegie Institution in Washington, the American Folklore Society, the American Museum of Natural History in New York, and the U.S. Bureau of American Ethnology—he selected thirty-six. Brown found stories representing the fun and good humor characteristic of the Native American. He chose legends attributed to twenty-one different tribes and organized them into nine broad categories such as Allegories, Tricksters and Magicians, Heroes and Heroines, Animal Stories, and Ghost Stories. Brown states, "The situations are universal, reminiscent of life as it goes on anywhere on this earth" (*Tepee*

Tales 10). Each section is introduced by a special illustration from Native American artist Louis Mofsie. This collection differs from many others in that Brown retells the stories as he thinks a modern-day English-speaking American Indian storyteller would present them. He eliminates archaic words and references, clarifies plots and meanings, and provides conclusions for some stories that were without endings. Brown's six pages of sources, dating from the 1880s to 1955, should be most helpful to anyone interested in learning about Indian legends.

Although Brown's extensive research gives his books authenticity, critics such as C.C. Loomis have found his dialogue "artificial; it flattens his characters" ("Brown, Dee," *Contemporary Authors* 94). In spite of that weakness in creating dialogue, Brown has three novels of considerable size and scope among his published books: *Creek Mary's Blood* (1980), *Killdeer Mountain* (1983), and *Conspiracy of Knaves* (1987).

The first of these three novels grew out of "a three-paragraph entry on a woman called Creek Mary who organized a group of male warriors and stormed Savannah in an attempt to drive out the British during the Revolutionary War" (Klemesrud 42). His interest piqued, Brown began the research for a novel built around a central character roughly modeled after Creek Mary, and he found that in two Indian tribes, the Creeks and the Cherokees, women were allowed to assume leadership roles, often by inheritance. His Creek Mary would be such a leader and would represent all Indians who suffered from the treacherous treatment of white governments. He gave her a tribal name of "Amayi."

Brown effectively uses the literary technique of flashback in recounting his Creek Mary's family history—a history that spans five generations and more than a century, from pre-revolutionary days until the turn of the nineteenth century. The novel opens in 1905 with Mary Dane, a young Indian woman from Montana, having lunch with President Theodore Roosevelt. She is being honored for her graduation from medical school, since she is the first of her race and sex to earn a medical degree. A newspaper reporter, who had once tried to trace the tale of Creek Mary, connects young Mary to his old interest and pursues his investigation. He travels to Montana to interview the young Mary's grandfather, ninety-year-old Dane, who is Creek Mary's grandson. The old Indian recounts to the reporter the past and present of the family saga and its endless unsuccessful encounters with the white man. He tells how the original Creek Mary was married successively to two men: a British trader, John Kingsley; and Long Warrior, a Cherokee chief. She had one son with each husband. The two husbands appear to symbolize two approaches to dealing with whites, Kingsley representing an attempt at assimilation and accommodation, Long Warrior standing for resistance. Both approaches to coexistence fail because Indians are powerless economically and politically and because the white man has a morality of convenience rationalized by Christianity.

The confrontations of Creek Mary and her family often end in defeat for the Indians. Because of the white man's greed and obsession with acquiring more and more land, Creek Mary's family can never find a place to settle permanently and are driven from Georgia and the Carolinas into Tennessee, then along the Trail of Tears, and finally, onto the Plains. The grandchildren of Creek Mary fight at Little Big Horn, slaying Custer's men, but are themselves massacred at Wounded Knee. The family line tenuously survives, and young Mary returns to the Montana reservation to give her people the best she has derived from the white culture.

Creek Mary's Blood stirred a great deal of response from reviewers and critics. Although Brown tried to speak from the Indian perspective, as he had done so successfully in *Bury My Heart at Wounded Knee* (1970), Leslie Marmon Silko felt that in his 1980 novel, "Dee Brown may understand how Indians perceive themselves in relation to the land, but he is unable to coax this view out of his Indian characters" (10). "What we are offered," she says, "is a non-Indian view of the world which [the author identifies] as Indian" (22). Joshua Gilder finds that "[Brown's] characters talk history to one another in an improbably self-conscious way" (76). Gilder also concludes, "Dee Brown . . . has turned fascinating savages into boring humanists" (77). Several reviewers found Brown's Creek Mary to be too modern. Robert Gish claims she is "unbelievably and anachronistically too androgynous, too assertive, too au courant, too much the total woman/man . . . " (B2). But *The New Yorker* reported, "This is the most successful combination of fact and fiction: the characters and their private dramas fit inside historical form as neatly as a nutmeat in its shell" (149).

In "The Historical Novel and *Creek Mary's Blood*," Ward Churchill strongly condemns Brown's novel, pointing out several historical inaccuracies in the text: the central character's name was changed, the Savannah march was really over a land dispute, and Mary's actual marriages and progeny differ substantially from those in the novel. Churchill also faults Brown for the manipulation of time to suit story development, and he contends that Brown creates a caricature of the real Creek Mary and reduces her to "an inept wanton whose primary motivation seemed to be the satisfaction of her physical desires" (127). Churchill apparently bases his information regarding Creek Mary upon the book *Indian Women Chiefs* (1966) by Caroline Thomas Foreman.

Yet Brown was aware of historical adjustments, as is evidenced by his statements to Judy Klemesrud in her April 1980 interview. He says, "I tried to make the historical events as accurate as possible, but I did make some changes for dramatic effect. That's something you never do in non-fiction, and I felt guilty about it. I'd change things a little bit and say, 'I can't do that.' then I would go and read other novels based on the past and say, 'They made changes, I'm going to do it, too' " (42). In the same interview, Brown indicates Creek Mary was married to a trader named Thomas Bosomworth, which is not a name in his novel but is one listed by Churchill as her third and last husband. Brown seems to be familiar with the historical Creek Mary, but he dramatized her story to tell his tale of an Indian family involved in all the major confrontations of their generations: the Trail of Tears, Little Big Horn, and Wounded Knee.

Paul Pavich finds "a number of minor problems with content and style," but he says that flaws in *Creek Mary's Blood* "do not negate its better qualities" (73). Pavich praises Brown's facility with English prose and credits him with drawing vivid scenes. In contrast, Silko felt Brown missed the mark, and she contends the works of non-Indian writers such as Frank Waters, Claire Huffaker, and Dan Cushman are more worthwhile and that Native American writers have produced far better novels (22). But Brown apparently had anticipated an objection like Silko's when he remarked that he thought *Creek Mary's Blood* would be his last book with an Indian as the main character. He also went on to say, "There's a whole new generation of Indians who can write beautifully. At least a dozen can write better than I can. . . . I think it's their turn now" (Klemesrud 42).

Killdeer Mountain (1983) was Brown's next novel. Set in the familiar time and place of the Western frontier of the post-Civil War era, *Killdeer* is nevertheless a departure from Brown's usual offering. It is a mystery story. A tangled web of intrigue results from mistaken identity (deliberate and accidental), distorted versions of events, confused memories, and ambiguous motivations.

As in *Creek Mary's Blood*, a reporter serves as the primary narrator. Sam Morrison of the *Saint Louis Herald* is dispatched up the Missouri River "in search of more stories of conflict and gore" (5), a cynical reference to appeasing the appetites of subscribers accustomed to years of war news. While Morrison is on his way to find lodging at a small hotel one stormy night, a shadowy figure intercepts him and sends him to a steamboat docked at a nearby pier. The ship's captain, who is an old wartime acquaintance of the reporter, welcomes him aboard. Five passengers, three women and two men, are introduced as the informants for the story that Morrison is about to hear. Another source of information, a businessman who was once an Army sergeant, is added at the ship's destination. This group is gathering to attend a ceremony naming a rebuilt fort in honor of a Major Charles Rawley, the son of a powerful Ohio senator. Major Rawley was presumed to have died in a fire that consumed the old fort. Morrison tries to put together a story about Rawley, gathering facts from his fellow travelers.

Here is where the confusion and contradictions begin. The several people each tell a different tale about preceding events. Some distortions are deliberate, some are merely misunderstandings of things seen and heard, but all of the tales contribute to obscuring the real story of Major Rawley. The known facts are that Rawley commanded a unit of Galvanized Yankees sent to protect gold-rush wagons. But Rawley's troop was ambushed by Indians at Killdeer Mountain, and there was only one survivor. Some say he was Rawley; others say he is Hardesty, one of the troopers who was an old friend of Rawley. The survivor later tells Morrison that he is Selkirk, a man married to Kathleen Martin, who also knew Rawley. This is the reporter's puzzle: is the man Rawley or Hardesty/Selkirk?

The survivor has told the Army that he is Rawley. He takes another troop on a raid, but he disobeys orders and the mission fails. When his court-martial trial is delayed, Rawley redeems himself by capturing a wanted Indian leader, Spotted Horse. Rawley claims a reward, which he gives to a sergeant and a woman. This couple buy hotels with the reward money and later turn up among the boat passengers. Although Rawley has been received as a hero for the capture, he knows his captive is really a peaceful old Indian, Medicine Horse, not the infamous Spotted Horse. Rawley arranges an escape for Medicine Horse, but the plot fails, and the fort burns in the process. A burned corpse is found and assumed to be Rawley. The major, Rawley-Hardesty/Selkirk, flees.

Joining the crowd at the fort dedication, Morrison sits next to Hardesty's widow. The man who fled the fort fire appears and disrupts the proceedings. Widow Hardesty claims it is her husband. Morrison confronts the man, who steadfastly maintains he is Rawley. All clues in the narrative thus far indicate the mystery man is really Hardesty. Morrison returns to St. Louis, unable to unravel the mystery. A year later, he meets the steamboat captain, who reports he has seen the man and Hardesty's widow living together as a couple named Selkirk. They were together in a saloon, singing a tune linked throughout the story with Kathleen and Drew Hardesty. The captain asks Morrison the man's real identity, but the reporter replies, "If you do not know him, sir, I can't say for certain who he is. Truthfully I don't know, but if I knew and told you the truth, you would never believe me" (279). And so the story ends.

Thus the reader is left with an indeterminate ending, the Lady or the Tiger choice. Jonathan Coleman complains that the conclusion of *Killdeer Mountain* is too open-ended and the reader is left exasperated (15). Stephen L. Tanner, however, has concluded that the book is "deliberately and ingeniously" constructed. He feels Brown is providing a look at frontier uniqueness: the use of shifting identities (1-10). This device is typical of much of Western American literature. Tanner refers to Huck Finn, the nicknames assumed by Bret Harte's characters, Owen Wister's Virginian, and Melville's Confidence Man (8). Tanner makes a strong case for the book having been intentionally and cleverly designed to end ambiguously. Clues are cunningly placed to mislead the reader, even with careful reading (7). Tanner also proposes that Brown may be reflecting a current preoccupation with indeterminacy in historical and critical theory (9).

As a historical researcher, Brown knows it is not always easy to ferret out the truth. Evidence may be ambiguous or nonexistent. Brown explains the basic philosophical assumption underlying the novel: "The world we view is a simple mirror that tricks us with false images so that what we believe to have happened . . . may or may not have taken place . . . " (1). Moreover, Brown reminds us that "life itself . . . is a mystery and not one of us is always who or what we seem to be" (2).

Leland DuVall claims Brown has written perhaps his best novel in *Killdeer Mountain* (3C), and Tanner found the book to be an engrossing Western adventure (10). *Publishers Weekly* faintly praises the book by noting that "altogether, it is a novel in which some parts are better than the whole" (70).

Brown followed up *Killdeer Mountain* with another novel with an involved plot, *Conspiracy of Knaves* (1987). The story line of *Knaves* has as its historical basis a Civil War event known as the Northwest Conspiracy. It concerned a complicated plan by a group of Copperheads (Northerners sympathetic to the Confederacy) and Confederate agents to free a group of Rebel prisoners held in Chicago. The released troops would then move on the Midwest and bring an end to the war. Brown introduces a female narrator, Belle Rutledge, who becomes a willing player in the Copperheads' drama. Belle is Brown's first attempt to use a female narrator.

Rutledge, a young actress from Kentucky, finds herself involved with individuals from both the Union and the Confederate sides during the Civil War and falls naturally into the role of double agent. She is an expedient person, totally lacking in idealism. Unfortunately, Brown missed a major opportunity by failing to develop the emotions and misplaced loyalties of the participants. Rutledge is allowed to function as a sort of self-indulgent Scarlett O'Hara. Others characters are generally dupes or swaggering adventurers. Belle falls in love with one handsome rogue, but ends up at home in Kentucky with another faithful fellow and settles into a quiet life, although not entirely free of her dreams. The Civil War ends and most of the conspirators are pardoned and go their individual ways—some to further adventure and others to pick up the pieces of their old lives.

The nature of the story-line of *Knaves* allows for high adventure, intrigue, excitement, and romance. The inherent drama is sometimes slowed, however, when Brown imparts some of his vast knowledge of the time and place he depicts. The insertion of many actual pertinent historical events such as the excursions of Morgan's Raiders, escapes to Canada, and military trials at Fort Douglas gives credence to the story, but it also sometimes intrudes upon the action. Nevertheless, *Knaves* contains enough suspense and continuity to hold a reader's interest in spite of not fully exploring the motives and sympathies of the many characters.

Each of Brown's three major novels had its genesis in an obscure document or report. *Creek Mary's Blood* grew from an account of a woman leading a band of warriors against British troops. *Killdeer Mountain* evolved from a government report concerning the burning of a frontier fort. *Conspiracy of Knaves* was based on another government document containing the complete proceedings of a trial of Civil War conspirators. Yet beyond their similarity in having historical sources as initial inspiration, the books differ markedly in purpose. *Creek Mary* dramatizes the despoliation of the countryside and the destruction of Indian culture by the white man. A mystery story, *Killdeer* has no apparent purpose beyond weaving a complex plot and challenging its audience to untangle the threads. In *Knaves*, Brown shows the involvement of women in the Civil War, as well as the variety of forces at work away from the battlefields. Regardless of his purpose, in each novel he conveys a lasting impression of the time and events.

Over his nearly fifty years as a writer, this talent for conveying a strong impression of historical events and eras, whether the canvas has been broad or limited, is what has emerged as Dee Brown's strength. He is most acclaimed for the diligent research and careful documentation of his non-fiction, particularly the much honored *Bury My Heart at Wounded Knee* (1970). But he has also written a number of other non-fiction works, including *Fort Phil Kearny* (1962), a detailed account of the Fetterman massacre; *Galvanized Yankees* (1963), a look at the activities of captured Confederate soldiers paroled to duty on the Indian frontier; *The Westerners* (1974), a handsomely illustrated survey of the exploration of the West; *Hear That Lonesome Whistle Blow* (1977), the story of the building of the transcontinental railroads; *Year of the Century* (1966), a series of sketches of the panorama of life in the centennial year of the United States.

Brown marked another anniversary in 1982. He put together a small volume, *The American Spa: Hot Springs, Arkansas* (1982), to honor that city's one hundred fiftieth year. He recalls that during research for this book, he found a fascinating old newspaper report about the place by a then-unknown reporter named Stephen Crane. Such a fortuitous discovery typifies the serendipity that often accompanies Brown's research. He feels it has been almost uncanny the way fascinating documents have come swimming into his hands (Courtemanche-Ellis 552).

After Brown has examined documents related to a particular subject, he generally continues to write about that subject in subsequent books and articles. Of the books mentioned above, *Fort Phil Kearny: An American Saga* (1962) is the one whose subject matter most often resurfaces in Brown's work. This book presents a thoroughly documented chronicle of the Fetterman massacre, a major tactical victory by the Indians on the Wyoming frontier. The chronological chapter headings correspond to Indian markings, which use moons of the different seasons such as the "Moon When Geese Lay Eggs," and which provide a logical structure for the development of the story. Brown takes the reader step by step through the details of the establishment of the fort. He explores the personality and character of the leading participants, Commandant Colonel Henry B. Carrington and Captain William J. Fetterman, who led the eighty-one-man detail that was ambushed by a combined force of Sioux, Cheyenne, and Arapaho warriors under Red Cloud. No troopers survived. Carrington contended that Fetterman had disobeyed explicit orders, and the disastrous results went beyond the immediate loss of lives in the field. The massacre destroyed the career and life of Colonel Carrington and resulted in the immediate abandoning of the forts and routes through the Powder River country. Reviewer Don Russell felt that *Fort Phil Kearny* was "one of the best studies made of any sector of the Indian wars" (6).

The narrative style of *Fort Phil* allows the actions and words of the participants to tell the story without the interjection of the author's interpretation. Brown uncovered some of the documented material in this book when he was doing the research for *Fighting Indians of the West* (1948). He included in *The Gentle Tamers* (1958) the diaries and personal correspondence of Frances Grumman, the widow of one of the Fetterman unit's officers. Brown suggests in *Fort Phil* the tragedy of all the Indian wars of the West that he later explores more completely in *Bury My Heart* (1970) and *Creek Mary's Blood* (1980). Nevertheless, in *Fort Phil* he writes a riveting report of a tragic blunder.

The Galvanized Yankees (1963) depicts action on the same frontier as that of *Fort Phil Kearny*, but Brown confines his focus to the movements of soldiers known as "galvanized Yankees," a term applied to Confederate prisoners who, as an alternative to imprisonment, enlisted into the U.S. Volunteers for Western frontier duty. These men were organized into six regiments of about a thousand men each and functioned between September 1864 and November 1866. Brown had a particular interest in this group because he felt his grandfather Cranford had been a member of one of the units.

From his research for both *Fort Phil Kearny* and *Galvanized Yankees*, Brown uncovered materials concerning the influence of people in power and of those striving for power. He wondered how these individuals and events affected the tone of the United States' first century. In *The Year of the Century: 1876* (1966), Brown tries to capture the mood and sense of the country during that centennial year. He presents a series of vignettes and character sketches about such figures as Presidential candidates Rutherford B. Hayes and Samuel J. Tilden; the famed showman P.T. Barnum; the novelist Horatio Alger, Jr.; and Dwight L. Moody, a shoe salesman. President Grant gets favorable treatment in Brown's panorama of America's centennial year.

Although Brown looks at "the social, political, and cultural atmosphere of the United States in the decade following the Civil War" (Bevilacqua 144), he chooses to treat the issues in a lively, amusing, episodic format. But instead of noting Brown's usual accurate interpretation of carefully documented research, several reviewers complained that *The Year of the Century* "is sometimes very imprecise" (Bevilacqua 144). S.G. Heppell praises Brown's style: "The prose reads smoothly and swiftly with image-making qualities" (2834). Although it is an easily read overview of the spirit of confidence and exuberance marking 1876, some reviewers criticized *The Year of the Century* for inaccuracy.

Some of the powerful figures Brown learned about in his research for *The Year of the Century* had acquired their status through their connections with railroad development. And materials he had read for *Fort Phil Kearny* included considerable information about the influence of the expanding railroad systems upon the disruption of the traditional Indian hunting grounds. The building of the railroads across the West figured prominently in the conflicts of the Indian wars. While the establishment of outposts such as Fort Phil Kearny and Fort C.F. Smith along the Western frontier was for the purpose of securing the Bozeman Road across the Powder River hunting grounds, it also coincided with the entry of the Union Pacific into that country. The discovery of gold in Idaho in 1860 and in Montana in 1862 spurred the extension of rails toward those sites, and the first passengers rode the Union Pacific into Wyoming in 1867. These bits of information spurred Brown to write *Hear That Lonesome Whistle Blow: Railroads in the West* (1977).

A story not just of the heroic and dedicated rail builders, but also of the greedy, corrupt, and duplicitous rail promoters and their political allies, *Lonesome Whistle* focuses on the Union Pacific-Central Pacific line as a prototype. Denied access to the Union Pacific Railroad's archives, Brown relied on standard nineteenth-century historical sources such as individual state records, published railroad company histories, and contemporary articles and reports from travelers. *Lonesome Whistle* contains eight pages of notes and ten and one-half pages of bibliography.

Although amazed to discover just how many times over the American public has paid for a rail system that is inadequate at best, Brown had expected to find that great fortunes had been made by the rail barons, but he was not prepared for the discovery of the great expense and sacrifice visited upon those who did the actual work. *Lonesome Whistle* includes chapters not only about the Chinese and Irish and others who dug the tunnels and laid the rails but also about the board-room entrepreneurs and the bone-jarred riders of the system.

Some of the material expanded upon in *Lonesome Whistle* had been used earlier by Brown in writing *The Westerners* (1974). Chapter XI, "The Grandest Enterprise Under God," is a factual account of the individuals and events pertinent to the building of the Central Pacific and Union Pacific railroads from the Missouri River to the Pacific Ocean. In the bibliography of this one chapter, Brown lists over twenty documents, unpublished diaries, and published books. Detailed documentation like that of *Lonesome Whistle* also characterizes each of the seventeen chapters of *The Westerners*. Organized chronologically, these seventeen chapters tell the story of the American West through the experiences of a few representative Westerners, covering a time frame from the sixteenth century to the twentieth. The book is richly illustrated and *Choice* proclaims it "beautifully written" (284).

The opening chapter tells of the Spanish forays into the Southwest, and the final chapter covers the activities of Teddy Roosevelt as a cattle rancher in the Dakotas and as a Rough Rider during the Spanish-American War. The chapters in between follow a variety of well-known and lesser-known Western figures. Although their motives and interests varied, those representative Westerners contributed to the conquering of the vast unspoiled wilderness regions. Lewis and Clark, John Colter, Francis Parkman, Brigham Young, Sitting Bull, the Custers, and dozens of other rugged individuals are among the historical personages *The Westerners* features.

In his introduction for this book, Brown writes that "The story of the American West has all the elements of the *Iliad* and *Odyssey*," and he adds that "Only an epic poet, a Homer, could encompass the American West and sing its essence into one compact volume" (7). He thus acknowledges that *The Westerners* is but an attempt to present some small measure of that essence. Bernard DeVoto, who included several of the same frontier figures in his works and managed a more complete presentation, is a more vivid writer than Brown and displays a more acute sense of the dramatic. Yet DeVoto and Brown share a journalistic background and the journalist's instinct for what makes a good story. They naturally gravitate to similar stylistic devices: quotations from letters and personal journals; replication of old newspaper clippings; episodic organization. DeVoto and Brown both write fiction and history, and each has been praised by reviewers more for his works of history, although each is a talented storyteller.

Although it does not achieve the vividness and dramatic intensity of De Voto's histories, *The Westerners* is a fine piece of work, well-organized, sensitively written, and profusely illustrated. Yet it lacks the emotional appeal of *Bury My Heart* and thus did not achieve the popular success of that book.

Actually, Brown himself was surprised at the overwhelming acceptance of *Bury My Heart at Wounded Knee* (1970). He told Lila Freilicher, "I never expected this . . . . In fact there were at least three of [my other books] that I had to put much more work into because I was still looking for sources. Yet nobody paid any attention to the others" (34). Because he hadn't altered his style or content, he remains mystified by the tremendous popular appeal of *Bury My Heart* (personal interview).

Published on 28 January 1971, *Bury My Heart* first appeared on the *New York Times* best seller list on March 14th. By April, it had gone into a fifth printing and the paperback rights were quickly purchased by Bantam for a reported six-figure sum (Freilicher 34).

In the introduction to *Bury My Heart*, Brown states that he chose for the time frame of the book the thirty-year span between 1860 and 1890 because this period provides "The greatest concentration of recorded experience and observation . . . . It was an incredible era of violence, greed, audacity, sentimentality, undirected exuberance, and an almost reverential attitude toward the ideal of personal freedom for those who already had it" (*xv*). He goes on to say, "During that time the culture and civilization of the American Indian was destroyed, and out of that time came virtually all the great myths of the American West" (*xv*).

The book contains no events that Brown had not covered in previous works. This time, however, everything is seen from the viewpoint of the Indian. Although Brown subtitled *Bury My Heart, An Indian History of the American West*, it would probably have been more accurate to follow the example of Helen Hunt Jackson, who had published similarly organized material in her *A Century of Dishonor* (1881): she labeled her book a series of sketches, not a history. Jackson felt a true history would require a full-book treatment for each episode. Her treatise seems to have been based on many of the same official records and reports researched by Brown; but having been politically active on behalf of the Indian cause, she included in her work a legal defense of Indian actions and took what was admittedly an emotional approach to gain public support. Brown chose to let the material speak for itself. He also had the advantage of later references sympathetic to the Indians such as the works of Hamlin Garland and Mari Sandoz. These are cited in the notes for *Bury My Heart.*

Brown's sources for this carefully documented and designed work were substantial: official records, diaries, pictographs, memoirs, unpublished letters and papers, nineteenth-century newspapers, treaty council records, contemporary interviews (eye-witness accounts), and words from such Indian leaders as Chief Joseph, Geronimo, and Crazy Horse. His listed notes and bibliography confirm Brown's claim that he could support everything in *Bury My Heart* with a document. He had collected these materials over the twenty-five years prior to writing *Bury My Heart* and had spent most of his spare time in the late 1960s reviewing them (*Current Biography* 54).

Bury My Heart consists of nineteen chapters. After the first chapter presents a brief overview of the decline and destruction of Indian tribes and their lands, each succeeding chapter details the specific treatment and experience of an individual tribe. Each tribe's leaders either died in the conflict with whites or ended up in captivity; and Brown describes the sad state of tribal survivors. The Navaho, Sioux, Cheyennes, Oglala, Arapaho, Apaches, Modocs, Utes, and Nez Percés are all main characters in the final stage of the white man's conquest of the West. The book does not ignore the acts of Indians killing whites, but in context, these acts are seen as generally retaliatory. They occur in response to an invasion of tribal grounds or the destruction of tribal property or the slaying of tribal members. There are also groups of frustrated, uncontrolled renegade warriors who rampage wantonly. The final chapter of the book tells the story of what happened at Wounded

Knee on 29 December 1890 when Big Foot and the remnants of his band were massacred while under escort to the Pine Ridge Reservation. It was the last act in a drama that had begun in 1876 at Little Big Horn. Somewhere along that same Wounded Knee Creek has been buried the heart of the great war chief, Crazy Horse, who had been killed at Fort Robinson on 5 September 1877 while under arrest.

The last battles of Crazy Horse are related in Chapter Twelve, titled "The War for the Black Hills." Each chapter of *Bury My Heart* can be read independently, but the book has an overall chronological organization. Chapter headnotes list various historical events of that period and set the stage for what follows. Pertinent treaties and quotes from tribal leaders precede the chapter narrative. The headnotes to Chapter Twelve contain a quote from Crazy Horse: "One does not sell the earth upon which the people walk" (273). The headnotes, which also list the words of twelve other chiefs regarding the Black Hills, then present an excerpt from the Treaty of 1868 promising Indian sovereignty of the territory. Chapter Thirteen, "The Flight of the Nez Percés," is preceded by a statement from Yellow Wolf of that tribe: "The whites told only one side. Told it to please themselves. Told much that is not true. Only his own best deeds, only the worst deeds of the Indians, has the white man told" (316). The sincerity of the Indian words, the ethics and logic, the accommodation of all life forms, the expressions of betrayal contained in those words, all establish the unifying theme of *Bury My Heart*: injustice to the Indian.

A good measure of the strength and impact of *Bury My Heart* may be attributed to the straight factual reportorial narrative counterpointing the eloquent and poignant speeches of the Indian leaders. When relating the killing of Crazy Horse, Brown writes, "The scuffling went on for only a few seconds. Someone shouted a command,

and then the soldier guard, Private William Gentles, thrust his bayonet deep into Crazy Horse's abdomen" (312). The prose is simple and straightforward, without emotional embellishment. The passage continues, "Crazy Horse died that night, September 5, 1877, at the age of thirty-five. At dawn the next day the soldiers presented the dead chief to his father and mother" (312).

The tolerance and restraint shown by most of the tribal chieftains are remarkable in the face of the indignities visited upon their peoples by the invading white men under the excuse of Manifest Destiny. The Indians consistently waived their rights of possession and demonstrated a willingness to share the lands and bounty of America until they felt they had nothing left to share. From the viewpoint of the Indians, they had tried to keep their promises and to accept the ways of the white man. Captain Jack, Kintpuash of the Modocs, says in part, "I have always told the white man heretofore to come and settle in my country; that it was his country and Captain Jack's country. That they come and live there with me and that I was not mad with them . . . . I have always [lived] peaceably and never asked any man for anything" (219).

Many Indians were reduced to treachery against their own. Little Big Man, who had fought beside Crazy Horse, helped arrest him (312). Given the white man's fear and denunciation of the last Indian religious movement, the Ghost Dance, it is ironical that the Ghost Dance beliefs were rooted in Christian beliefs and carried a message of peace and love. But because it provided hope and a unifying force, the Ghost Dance was perceived to be threatening to Western settlement and, as a result of that perception, its followers were destroyed.

Bury My Heart is important in the field of Western American history because, as Peter Farb asserts, the book "dispels any illusions that may still exist that the Indian wars were civilization's missions or Manifest Destiny: the Indian wars are shown to be the dirty murders they were" (36). Moreover, *Bury My Heart* recounts how the white man finally obliterated the red man and "won the West" at the expense of a powerless entity. Because the book is told from the point of view of the Indians—the victims—Helen McNeil considers *Bury My Heart* to be "a deliberately revisionist history [that tells] the story of the Plains Indians from an amalgamated Indian viewpoint, so that the westward march of the civilized white man . . . appears as a barbaric rout of established Indian culture" (444). Yet Cecil Eby expressed reservations regarding the scope of *Bury My Heart*: "Despite its solid research and original approach, this book is burdened by too many episodes and too many characters." He also noted: "The massacre at My Lai is brought uncomfortably closer to home" (3). N. Scott Momaday viewed *Bury My Heart* as "extraordinary on several accounts . . . so much of great drama and moment actually took place in the three decades of this remarkable story." Momaday, too, sees that "Having read Mr. Brown, one has a better understanding of what it is that nags at the American conscience at times . . . and of that morality which informs and fuses events so far apart in time and space as the massacres at Wounded Knee and My Lai" (47).

Tom Wallace, Brown's editor at Holt, Rinehart, thinks that a collective sadness about the violence of Americans at My Lai and in Vietnam in general probably contributed to the quick success of *Bury My Heart*. Elliott Arnold and Geoffrey Wolff also mentioned the Vietnam connection (Freilicher 34). Wallace also felt that enthusiastic advance comments, the number of excellent reviews, and a timely wave of interest in books by and about the American Indian helped put *Bury My Heart* on the best-seller list (Freilicher 34). There was, in fact, concurrent heightened public sensitivity to several minority movements, including those of African Americans and women.

With that heightened sensitivity, readers were especially moved by the Indians' eloquence in *Bury My Heart*. The Indians' speeches were mostly taken from government records of treaty proceedings and from field reports and were subject to the understanding and integrity of translators, some of whom were more competent than others. The imagery employed by the Indian chieftains, imagery consistent with their oral tradition, posed some problems for the more literal-minded recorders, but they soon adjusted to the Indians' delivery and captured the dignity and formality of the proceedings. Indeed, Lawrence C. Wroth feels that the treaty conference records constitute an original type of American literature (749-66). By making this moving literature available to the general reader, Brown insured that the Indians' story would become part of the national consciousness.

The actual writing of *Bury My Heart* took Brown slightly over two years, working nights. He was still on staff at the University of Illinois library during the daytime. He only guesses at the years spent collecting the documents. No reviewers challenged the accuracy of *Bury My Heart,* so Brown apparently succeeded in achieving the historical accuracy that he says has always been his goal: "In the non-fiction I have always attempted to dramatize the true events, using the tools of the novelist (diaries and letters are splendid for inner thought and stream of consciousness) but always aiming not to violate the rules of historical writing" (Bloodworth 121-22).

Brown shares an attitude expressed in detail and discussed at length by Wallace Stegner: "History, a fable agreed upon, is not a science but a branch of literature" (205). Stegner further states, "dramatizing of legitimately dramatic true events does not necessarily falsify them, nor need it leave their meaning ambiguous. Dramatic narrative is simply one means by which a historian can make a point vividly" (205). *Bury My Heart* successfully blends true events and dramatic narrative. Its sales have exceeded half a million hardback copies, and it continues to be assigned for college classes on Indian history. It is still in print two decades after publication.

During an authorial career of nearly half a century, Dee Brown has written for about every type of publication sold. In addition to his books, he has turned out newspaper columns, book reviews, essays, articles for popular magazines and for academic journals, and editorials. In the 1960s, he contributed to *Civil War Times*; in the 1970s, to *American History Illustrated*; and in the 1980s, he wrote frequent long articles for *Southern Magazine*. Brown appreciates the latitude of interpretation allowed in fiction, but asserts he is grateful for the discipline imposed by non-fiction. He credits that discipline with helping him structure his books (personal interview).

In his fiction, Brown uses literary devices similar to those of Western writer Will Henry, who establishes credibility by introducing his stories through a found diary or family papers (Koury 113). In his reliance upon documented materials, Brown differs from Oliver La Farge, another Western writer noted for his books about Indians. La Farge's romantic Indian fiction depends more upon personal experiences and observation (Gillis 570). All three writers, however, exhibit their love of Western lore.

Brown also shares the ambition of many Western writers to go beyond the old formula plots. He cites Walter Van Tilburg Clark's *The Ox-Bow Incident*, A. B. Guthrie, Jr.'s *The Way West*, and Charles Portis' *True Grit* as leading examples of Western historical novels that rise above the old formulas. He feels only a few authors of Westerns have been truly successful in breaking through the constraints of popular convention, but he finds the pursuit of this goal stimulating (personal interview). And he also finds great satisfaction in having pleased readers and at the same time having imparted to them a great deal of information about Fort Phil Kearny, an early Army Balloon Corps, Beecher Island, Galvanized Yankees, a genuine Davy Crockett, the environmental considerations and dignity of Indian cultures, the courage of settlers, men and women, the social consequences of the westward movement, and the heroics of great and small.

Most importantly, Brown has spoken out against injustice in many forms. When he felt Western women were not sufficiently recognized, he wrote of their worth. He recognized despoiling of the land and condemned it long before such a cause was popular. He also condemned the greed and personal aggrandizement of powerful and public figures.

In short, Dee Brown's very long and productive career has established him as an author of merit. His works have been translated into twenty languages and are still sold in many foreign countries. And *Bury My Heart* will remain a popular presentation of the genocide attendant to the winning of the West.

Brown's peers have recognized his contributions to Western American literature. He has been awarded a number of prizes: The American Library Association's Clarence Day Award, the New York Westerners' Buffalo Award, the Christopher Award, the Western Writers of America's Saddleman Award; and in 1984, the Award of Merit conferred by the American Association for State and Local History, citing forty years of cumulative contributions. In 1972 he was named Illinoisan of the Year by the Illinois Broadcaster's Association. The University of Central Arkansas (Arkansas State Teachers College) honored him in 1988 as Distinguished Alumnus of the Year, and the *Arkansas Times* magazine named him a 1988 Arkansas Hero in the second year of that award. But in spite of all these awards, Dee Brown has been a much underrated writer, because the extent of his research and acquired knowledge has been hidden by his apparently simple presentations.

Vine Deloria, Jr., asked Brown for an essay for a book he was editing to memorialize the poet John G. Neihardt. In the essay he contributed to the volume, Brown acknowledges the tremendous impact that Neihardt's poetry and vivid images had upon him. A college sophomore when he discovered Neihardt's work, Brown was forever impressed. He tells us in his essay that "It was as if I were following [as a writer] a well-marked pathway designed by a pioneer trail blazer, although I was not conscious of the fact that I was doing so at the time I chose to write the books" (10). While writing *Bury My Heart at Wounded Knee*, he felt the voice of Neihardt mixed in with Indian voices speaking in poetic prose. Brown concludes that he "heard it said that on the day John Neihardt died, a hawk came out of the West and circled his house three times and then flew away toward the setting sun" (11). Dee Alexander Brown continues to address his audience, but when at last his voice has been stilled, he will have earned his own circling hawk.

Selected Bibliography

PRIMARY SOURCES

Books by Brown

Action at Beecher Island. Garden City, New York: Doubleday, 1967. Rpt. New York: Dell, 1989.

The American Spa: Hot Springs, Arkansas. Little Rock: Rose, 1982.

Andrew Jackson and the Battle of New Orleans. New York: Putnam, 1972.

The Bold Cavaliers: Morgan's 2nd Kentucky Cavalry Raid. Philadelphia: Lippincott, 1959.

Bury My Heart at Wounded Knee: An Indian History of the American West. New York: Holt, 1970.

Cavalry Scout. New York: Permabooks, 1958. Rpt. New York: Dell, 1989.

Conspiracy of Knaves. New York: Holt, 1987.

Creek Mary's Blood. New York: Holt, 1980.

The Fetterman Massacre: An American Saga. London: Barrie, 1972.

Fighting Indians of the West. With Martin L. Schmitt. New York: Scribner's, 1948.

Fort Phil Kearny: An American Saga. New York: Putnam, 1962.

The Galvanized Yankees. Urbana: U of Illinois P, 1963.

The Gentle Tamers: Women of the Old West. New York: Putnam, 1958.

The Girl from Fort Wicked. Garden City, NY: Doubleday, 1964. Rpt. New York: Dell, 1989.

Grierson's Raid. Urbana: U of Illinois P, 1954.

Hear That Lonesome Whistle Blow. New York: Holt, 1977.

James L. Reid: The Man and His Corn. Urbana: U of Illinois P, 1955.

Killdeer Mountain. New York: Holt, 1983.

Pawnee, Blackfoot & Cheyenne. Ed. New York: Scribner's, 1960.

The Settlers' West. With Martin L. Schmitt. New York: Scribner's, 1955.

Showdown at Little Bighorn. New York: Putnam, 1964. Rpt. New York: Dell, 1988.

Tales of the Warrior Ants. New York: Putnam, 1973.

Tepee Tales of the American Indian. New York: Holt, 1979.
They Went Thataway. New York: Putnam, 1960. Reissued as *Pardon My Pandemonium* by August House, Little Rock, Arkansas, in 1984.
Trail Driving Days. With Martin L. Schmitt. New York: Scribner's, 1952.
Wave High the Banner. Philadelphia: Macrae-Smith, 1942.
The Westerners. New York: Holt, 1974.
The Year of the Century: 1876. New York: Scribner's 1966.
Yellowhorse. Boston: Houghton, 1956.

Articles by Brown

"Along the Santa Fe Trail." *American History Illustrated* Oct. 1980: 8-13.
"The Battle of Pea Ridge." *Civil War Times* (no vol. no.) 1967: 1-10.
"Butch Cassidy and the Sundance Kid." *American History Illustrated* June 1982: 57-63.
"Day of the Buffalo." *American History Illustrated* July 1976: 4-7.
"Day of the Longhorns." *American History Illustrated* Jan. 1976: 4-9.
"Farming in the Machine Age." *Christian Science Monitor* 24 Mar. 1937: 9.
"The First Environmentalist." *The New York Times* 15 June 1971: 13.
"Geronimo." *American History Illustrated* June 1980: 12-21; July 1980: 36-45.
"Growing Up in Arkansas Leaves Its Mark on Young Writer." *Arkansas Gazette* 14 June 1986: 19A.
"Historical Fiction, Its Infinite Variety." *The Writer* Oct. 1983: 11-14.
"Intrigue on the Natchez Trace." *Southern Magazine* Nov. 1986: 43-44, 74, 88.
"Legends of the Confederate Gold." *Southern Magazine* Nov. 1987: 49-51; 88-90.
"Perspectives on the Past." *American History Illustrated* June 1979: 18-20.
"Pony Express." *American History Illustrated* Nov. 1976: 4-7.
"The Power of John Neihardt." *A Sender of Words, Essays in Memory of John G. Neihardt.* Ed. Vine Deloria, Jr. Salt Lake City: Howe Brothers, 1984. 5-11.
"In Pursuit of Revenge." *American History Illustrated* Aug. 1981: 26-37.

"The Settlement of the Great Plains." *American History Illustrated* June 1974: 4-11.

WORKS CITED AND OTHER MATERIALS ABOUT BROWN

"Action at Beecher Island." Review in *Publishers Weekly* 23 Aug. 71: 82.

Bevilacqua, Winifred F. "Dee Brown." *Dictionary of Literary Biography Yearbook 1980*. Detroit: Gale, 1980. 143-47.

Bettersworth, J. K. Review of *Grierson's Raid*. *New York Times Book Review* 5 Dec. 1954: 26.

Birney, Hoffman. Review of *Fighting Indians of the West*. *New York Times Book Review* 7 Nov. 1948: 5.

Birney, Hoffman. Review of *Trail Driving Days*. *New York Times Book Review* 24 Feb. 1952: 18.

Birney, Hoffman. "Western Roundup." *New York Times Book Review* 9 Sept. 1956: VII, 26.

Bloodworth, William. "Dee Brown." *Twentieth Century Western Writers*. Ed. James Vinson and D. L. Kirkpatrick. Detroit: Gale, 1983.

"Bold Cavaliers." Review in *Kirkus* 1 Aug. 1959: 585.

Bold, Christine. *Selling the Wild West. Popular Fiction, 1860-1960*. Bloomington: Indiana UP, 1987.

Brown, Dee. "Growing Up in Arkansas Leaves Its Mark on a Young Writer." *Arkansas Gazette* 14 June 1986: 19A.

Brown, Dee. "Historical Fiction, Its Infinite Variety." *The Writer* Oct. 1983: 11-14.

Brown, Dee. "The Power of John Neihardt." *A Sender of Words, Essays in Memory of John G. Neihardt*. Ed. Vine Deloria, Jr. Salt Lake City: Howe Brothers, 1984. 5-11.

"Brown, Dee." *Contemporary Authors*. Detroit: Gale, 1984.

"Brown, Dee." *Current Biography*. New York: Wilson, 1979.

"Brown, Dee." Personal Interview. 10 Nov. 1980; 15 Mar. 1985; 7 Aug. 1988; 15 Oct. 1988; 20 June 1989; 7 Sept. 1989.

"Bury My Heart at Wounded Knee." Review in *Choice* 8 June 1971: 604.

Churchill, Ward. "The Historical Novel and *Creek Mary's Blood.*" *The Journal of Ethnic Studies* 12.3 (1984): 119-28.

Coleman, Jonathan. "Atoning for an Act of Mercy." *New York Times Book Review* 5 June 1983: 15.

Courtemanche-Ellis, Anne. "Dee Brown Arkansas Writer/Librarian." *Arkansas Libraries* 34.1 (1977): 8-17.

Courtemanche-Ellis, Anne. "Meet Dee Brown: Author/Teacher/Librarian." *Wilson Library Bulletin* Mar. 1978: 551-61.

"Creek Mary's Blood." Review in *The New Yorker* 7 Apr. 1980: 149.

"Dee Brown, Arkansas Hero." *Arkansas Times* Nov. 1988: 57.

DuVall, Leland D. " 'Killdeer Mountain': Intrigue on the Frontier." *Arkansas Gazette* 24 Apr. 1983: 3C.

Eby, Cecil. Review of *Bury My Heart. Book World* 28 Feb. 1971: 3.

Engle, Paul. Review of *Wave High the Banner. Saturday Review of Literature* 20 May 1942: 9.

Farb, Peter. Review of *Bury My Heart. New York Review of Books* 16 Dec. 1971: 36.

Farnham, W. D. Review of *The Galvanized Yankees. Journal of American History* 51 (1964): 502.

Freilicher, Lila P. " 'Bury My Heart at Wounded Knee.' " (The Story Behind the Book.) *Publishers Weekly* 19 Apr. 1971: 34-35.

French, Philip. Review of *Hear That Lonesome Whistle Blow. New Statesman* 30 Sept. 1977: 451.

"Gentle Tamers." Review in *Kirkus* 1 Feb. 1958: 111.

Gilder, Joshua. "Who's on First." *New York Magazine* 7 Apr. 1980: 76-77.

Gillis, Everett. "Oliver La Farge." *A Literary History of the American West.* Ed. J. Golden Taylor. Fort Worth: Texas Christian UP, 1987. 570.

Gish, Robert. Review of *Creek Mary's Blood. Christian Science Monitor* 10 Mar. 1980: B2.

Hayward, H. S. Review of *Hear That Lonesome Whistle Blow. Christian Science Monitor* 21 June 1977: 26.

Heppell, S. G. Review of *The Year of the Century: 1876. Library Journal*

1 June 1966: 2834.

Jackson, Helen Hunt. *A Century of Dishonor.* New York: Harper, 1881.

Jefferson, Margo. Review of *Hear That Lonesome Whistle Blow. Newsweek* 23 May 1977: 87.

"Killdeer Mountain." Review in *Publishers Weekly* 14 Jan. 1983: 70.

Klemesrud, Judy. "Behind the Best Sellers." *New York Times Book Review* 13 Apr. 1980: 42.

Koury, Michael. "The Military." *A Literary History of the American West.* Ed. J. Golden Taylor. Fort Worth: Texas Christian UP, 1987. 113.

La Farge, Oliver. Review of *Fighting Indians of the West. New York Herald Tribune Weekly Review* 1 Nov. 1948: 6.

Lewis, Bill. "Female Narrator, A First for Author." *Arkansas Gazette* 25 Jan. 1987: 8C.

McNeil, Helen. Review of *Bury My Heart. New Statesman* 1 Oct. 1971: 444.

McClellan, Joseph. "Following the Trail of Tears." *The Washington Post* 16 Mar. 1980: 5.

Momaday, N. Scott. Review of *Bury My Heart. New York Times Book Review* 7 Mar. 1971: 46-47.

Overton, R. C. Review of *Union Pacific Country. Journal of American History* 58 (1972): 1029.

Pasztor, David. "Oh, Say It Ain't So, Davy." *The Columbian* (Vancouver, Wash.) 17 Aug. 1986: B1.

Pavich, Paul. Review of *Creek Mary's Blood. Western American Literature* 16 (1981): 73.

"Railroad Builders." Review in *Mississippi Valley Historical Review* 7 (1920): 158.

Russell, Don. Review of *Fort Phil Kearny. Chicago Sunday Tribune* 29 Apr. 1962: 6.

Saltz, Irwin. "Former Arkansan Tells How It Feels to Turn Out a Top-Notch Best Seller." *Arkansas Gazette* 20 June 1971: 9E:2.

Shiras, Ginger. "Dee Brown, Best Selling Author and SGA Alumnus." *Arkansas Gazette* 28 Oct. 1971: 13A.

Silko, Leslie Marmon. "They Were the Land's." *New York Times Book Review* 25 May 1980: 10, 22.

Stegner, Wallace. *The Sound of Mountain Water*. Garden City: Doubleday, 1969.

Stewart, E. I. Review of *The Galvanized Yankees*. *American Historical Review* July 1964: 1167.

Tanner, Stephen L. "Questions of Identity in Dee Brown's *Killdeer Mountain*." Paper delivered at the Western Literature Association Conference, Durango, Colorado, Oct. 1986.

Thomas, B. P. Review of *Grierson's Raid*. *Chicago Sunday Tribune* 12 Dec. 1954: 6.

"Trail Driving Days." Review in *The New Yorker* 1 Mar. 1952: 96.

"Trail Driving Days." Review in *Time* 18 Feb. 1952: 104.

Wallace, Margaret. Review of *Wave High the Banner*. *New York Times* 3 May 1942: 16.

"The Westerners." Review in *Choice* Apr. 1975: 284.

Woody, R. H. Review of *Grierson's Raid*. *American Historical Review* 60 (1955): 688.

Wroth, Lawrence C. "The Indian Treaty as Literature." *Yale Review* 17.4 (1928): 749-66. Rpt. in *Literature of the American Indians: Views and Interpretations*. Ed. Abraham Chapman. New York: Meridian-NAL, 1975. 324-37.